Original title:
Palm Shadows and Ocean Mist

Copyright © 2025 Creative Arts Management OÜ
All rights reserved.

Author: Lorenzo Barrett
ISBN HARDBACK: 978-1-80581-552-5
ISBN PAPERBACK: 978-1-80581-079-7
ISBN EBOOK: 978-1-80581-552-5

Enchanted Waters

In a splashy dance, the fish do sway,
Winking at kids who shout, "No way!"
Seagulls dive down, with snacks in sight,
Claiming the beach their feast tonight.

Turtles wear shades, they strut with pride,
On tiny surfboards, they ride the tide.
Crabs in a conga, with claws held high,
Chuckling at waves that say goodbye.

Horizon's Embrace

A sunburned man, with his hat askew,
Claims he's just trying to catch a view.
But sideways he tilts, like a leaning tree,
As gulls plot a plan for their next spree.

Flipping sunscreen like it's a game,
His nose turns red, but he'll take the blame.
The horizon giggles, a kid's delight,
With waves that tease till deep in the night.

Whirlwinds of Fern

In the breeze, the ferns do sway,
A dance-off rages, come what may.
Lizards bob heads, like they're in the mix,
Witness the chaos, oh, what a fix!

Leaves wear conga lines, quite the show,
As ants march by with a rhythmic flow.
Nature joins in, clapping along,
In this wild dance, nothing feels wrong.

The Breath of the Shore

Sandy toes wiggle, pure bliss they seek,
With giggles that echo, not a hint of meek.
A beach ball sails, like a kite in the sky,
Bouncing off heads as the seagulls fly.

Sunscreen fights, with a twist and a flail,
The chased bottle journeys like an epic tale.
Who knew fun lurked in the salty spray?
In laughter's embrace, we'll frolic and play.

Intertwined in Nature's Embrace

In a land where breezes tease the trees,
Laughter floats on salty air with ease.
The sun hits just right, a playful glow,
While crabs tap dance, putting on a show.

With coconut hats and drinks in hand,
We chase each other on the warm, soft sand.
A frisbee's flight, a friend's quick dodge,
We giggle and splash, like kids on a lounge.

Glistening Trails of Twilight Dreams

As twilight whispers secrets to the tide,
A penguin sneezes, it's tough to hide!
Sandcastles crumble in a fit of glee,
The ocean joins in, "Look at me!"

Frogs leap like dancers in tiny shoes,
Chasing fireflies while we sip on brews.
The stars wink down, share giggles, too,
While a dolphin juggles a beach ball, who knew?

Tropical Echoes

In the jungle, jokes bounce off the leaves,
Monkeys swing, pulling off funny heaves.
A toucan squawks, "Got any good puns?"
While lizards bask, counting their fun runs.

Hammocks sway, their gentle embrace,
As we clash spoons in a coconut race.
The chattering birds join our silly feud,
While iguanas judge us, aloof and rude.

Whispering Waves

The waves belly-laugh, they've seen it all,
Sand crabs hosting their annual ball.
We spin and twirl, our sunscreen a mess,
Trying to dance but failing, I confess!

Seagulls squawk, "Hey, you missed a spot!"
While we dive for treasure, lost in the plot.
A friendship forged in laughter's embrace,
In nature's wild rhythm, we find our place.

Veils of Mist and Memory

When mornings play hide and seek,
The sea sneezes pearls, so unique.
Seagulls gossip, with flair and cheer,
"Did you see the crab? He's found his gear!"

Waves dance in laughter, all aglow,
While fish flip their tails, putting on a show.
A sandwich once lost, beneath the foam,
Returned with a fish, saying, "Welcome home!"

Ferns and Fables in Twilight's Embrace

Under leaves, secrets giggle and play,
As fireflies flash their jokes on display.
"Why did the ferns refuse to yell?
They couldn't find their voice, so they fell!"

Whispers rise as shadows take flight,
Chasing down dreams in the fading light.
Mice in tuxedos dance on a log,
While crickets sing ballads, a musical fog.

Cradled by the Coastal Breeze

The breeze whispers softly, "What's in your bag?"
An octopus answered, "Don't call me a hag!"
Shells giggle as they roll on their sides,
Saying, "We're here for the beach-side rides!"

Napping chairs sway, in a silly embrace,
As flip-flops conspire to join the race.
A kite sneezes high, flying out of control,
While waves laugh, "Look! An aerial stroll!"

Fading Echoes of Summer Shores

Bubbles bounce from old sun hats,
While crabs in bow ties dance with spats.
"Why are sunburns so hard to miss?
They say I'm hot, but I'm really just bliss!"

The tide pulls laughter towards the sand,
With shells exchanging gossip, oh so grand.
A flip flop's lost, in a love affair,
Left wondering, "Is this my sole despair?"

Shadows Play at Waters' Edge

Waves wiggle as the sunlight prances,
Laughter dances in the sandy glances.
Footprints vanish like a shy guest,
As sea foam tickles at my request.

Seagulls squawk like they're in a show,
Trying to steal my snack, oh no!
Fish winking, thinking they're so sly,
While crabs in castles wave goodbye.

The Lingering Embrace of Daylight

Sunscreen drips like melted ice cream,
Children giggle, oh what a dream!
In the glow, they twist and whirl,
A flip-flop's fate in this vibrant swirl.

Napping turtles rock with style,
While dolphins teach a silly smile.
Coconuts roll down the beach,
Shouting, "Hey, come take a breach!"

Horizon Kissed by Soft Whispers

The sky blushes in a funny way,
Like it just saw something gone astray.
Waves crash loud like a stand-up show,
With every splash, the sea says, "Whoa!"

Sandcastles lean like they're quite tipsy,
While the tide's dance makes them all frisky.
Shells gossip secrets in hushed tones,
As the breeze tickles their little bones.

Tales of Driftwood and Wildflowers

Old driftwood tells tales, quite absurd,
Of adventures with a wandering bird.
Wildflowers laugh at their patchy growth,
Spreading pollen, making a merry oath.

Ants march by with a plan so grand,
Stealing crumbs from the party band.
A hiccup laughs from the sun's good cheer,
As day slips shyly into evening's sphere.

Chasing the Light

The sun is playing hide and seek,
As I trip over my own two feet.
With laughter spilling like lemonade,
I'm pretty sure I've lost my shade.

I wave at clouds as if they know,
The secrets of where jokers go.
The seagulls laugh at my big plan,
To catch the light, a shining tan.

But every time I turn around,
The glow just giggles, spins, and bounds.
It's like a dance that won't sit still,
The sun's a silly thrill to thrill!

So here I wiggle, twirl with glee,
Embracing beams that wish to flee.
With every step I take and stride,
I chase the rays, I won't divide.

Lost in Dimension

In a world where shadows tease,
I take a tumble, trip on leaves.
The sun has brought me to this place,
Where giggles bounce in endless space.

A mermaid hums, and then I trip,
I thought I'd join her wavy dip.
But now I'm tangled in a grin,
With seaweed pulling me back in.

Dimensions swirl, it feels so fine,
To sip sweet thoughts and sip on brine.
I wave to fishes with a wink,
While juggling bubbles on the brink.

So here I float, without a care,
In a dimension quite so rare.
The laughter echoes, twists, and bends,
A place where fun will never end!

Rippled Wanderings

I set out on a goofy quest,
To find the waves that like to jest.
The ocean's tickle makes me squeal,
As sea foam wraps around my heel.

With every ripple, I must dance,
Although it seems I have no chance.
The tide winks back like old pals do,
While pelicans sing a silly tune.

But wait! What's that? A splashy spot!
A jellyfish, now that's a plot!
I leap away, oh what a sight,
And end up laughing in delight.

So wander on through waters wide,
With giggles spilling like the tide.
These rippled jaunts, a funny show,
Will have you laughing, don't you know?

The Horizon's Whisper

The edge of day begins to tease,
With whispers carried on the breeze.
It tickles ears, and here I stand,
A goofball in this golden land.

The sky leans down and gives a grin,
As if to say, 'Come dance and spin!'
I twirl with clouds, a silly race,
Ignoring all the serious face.

Yet deep below, the waves complain,
'Hey, stop that, we can't refrain!'
A fish appears with a big laugh,
And joins me in this playful path.

With every step toward dusk's delight,
The horizon shimmers, gleams so bright.
So let the whispers wind and flow,
In laughter's glow, we'll steal the show!

Sunlight Through the Foliage

Leaves giggle in the breeze,
Squirrels dance among the trees.
Sunbeams play hide and seek,
While the birds sing tunes so sleek.

A lizard dons a tiny hat,
Winks as if he thinks he's fat.
We laugh at shadows on the floor,
A daytime show we can't ignore.

Breezy whispers tickle our ears,
Tick-toeing past our sun-soaked fears.
Who would dare to stomp so loud?
Watch out! The ants are quite proud!

Jellybeans rain from the sky,
While grasshoppers leap and fly.
Nature's stage is set to please,
With silly sights and sunny breeze.

Ocean's Embrace

Waves that dance, oh what a sight,
Seagulls squawk, giving us a fright.
Buckets spill with laughter's gleam,
As crabs join in the building team.

Sandy toes and sunburned nose,
Jumping in without a pose.
A fishy friend steals my snack,
With a laugh, I chase him back.

The tide will roll and waves will crash,
As kids all giggle with a splash.
Shells lined up like tiny cars,
Prompting dreams of ocean stars.

Sandcastles wear a silly crown,
As waves come knocking them down.
Amidst the fun, we lose all haste,
In ocean's arms, we find our taste.

Mirage of Tranquility

On a hammock, I sway, oh what bliss,
The world speeds by; I steal a kiss.
Giggly geckos, oh so spry,
On this wobbly ride, we fly high.

A dream of cake floats in the air,
While gentle breezes tangle my hair.
Coconut crabs play peekaboo,
With every glance, it feels brand new.

Palm leaves rustle, whispering rhymes,
With clock hands stuck at silly times.
The sun begins its cheeky dance,
As everyone joins in the chance.

Floating thoughts that jostle my head,
Tickling ideas, I laugh instead.
A mirage of laughter, sunshine, and cheer,
In this world, we hold dear.

Lullabies of the Lagoon

Fireflies tango in twilight's gleam,
Crickets strum a nighttime theme.
As frogs croak jokes from their spot,
The moon rolls in, oh what a plot.

Giggly fish in a sparkling show,
Boogie-woogie across the flow.
Stars twinkle with mirthful glee,
Joining in on the jubilee.

Drifting dreams on a water slide,
Children laughing, open wide.
The trees share tales of giggles past,
In this lagoon, we find love vast.

With each ripple, we sway and sway,
A lullaby leads us astray.
Serenades that tickle our hearts,
In a world where laughter never departs.

The Edge of Solitude

On a beach where seagulls dive,
A hermit crab takes a wild jive.
He sidesteps left, then right, then spins,
In a shell that makes him look like wins.

The waves come in, they tickle his toes,
He giggles loud, then quickly goes.
With each splash, he dances anew,
Who knew crabs could be silly too?

Shells and laughter fill the sand,
A conch shell's tune, he starts a band.
The sun sets low, but spirits rise,
Who wouldn't laugh at this surprise?

With sand between his tiny feet,
Even crabs find life so sweet.
As twilight whispers, crabs unite,
For a moonlit party, pure delight.

Gentle Ripples of Dusk

A duck wearing shades, what a sight,
Flapping wings, he takes to flight.
He quacks a tune, off-key and loud,
In his own world, he feels so proud.

The tide comes in, but he won't mind,
He paddles fast, relaxation, he'll find.
With every splash, a giggling croak,
Life's a joke, and he's the bloke.

Seagulls swoop by, give him a cheer,
"Hey, cool duck, come join us here!"
But he just grins, and shakes it off,
With a wink, he leads a silly scoff.

As the sun dips low and colors blend,
Our duck now struts, he knows no end.
In the dusk, he rules the lake,
A quacking star, make no mistake!

Serenity's Caress

A cat in a hammock, snoozing away,
Dreams of fish in the light of the day.
It rolls and tumbles in seas of cream,
Not a care in the world, just a soft dream.

Nearby, a dog, with a mischievous bark,
Keeps watch on the tail of a lizard in park.
Every time it leaps, the dog leaps too,
Chasing laughs and giggles, like it's brand new.

The sun dips down, and shadows chase,
As our kitty awakes with a silly face.
A nap was great, but now it's time,
To join in the antics, it's simply sublime.

With wagging tails and purring delight,
Together they bring the twilight bright.
In a world where silliness has no end,
To the edge of fun, all creatures blend.

The Secret of the Sea

A hermit crab hides a snack in his shell,
He thinks no one knows. Oh, can't you tell?
When the waves crash in and the gulls start to squawk,
He munches his chips while taking a walk.

A fish swims by, wearing a cap,
Asking, "Hey buddy, mind if I nap?"
But the crab just laughs and offers a fry,
"Join me for dinner, and let's not be shy!"

Under the waves, where the barnacles cling,
An octopus shows off his whole bling-bling.
With a wink and a smile, he flashes his loot,
"We're the best underwater comedy troupe!"

As the sunset glimmers on waves gone wild,
The ocean snickers, like a playful child.
In this secret realm where fun never flees,
Who knew laughter was the key to the seas?

The Lure of Dappled Drift

Beneath the trees, a prankster waits,
With wobbly legs and funny fates.
He trips on roots and starts to laugh,
As sunlight dances on his path.

A cheeky crab joins in the fun,
With sideways steps, he's on the run.
They race along the sandy shore,
Chasing shadows, wanting more.

Seagulls squawk with playful glee,
Diving down for a chance to see.
Everyone whispers, 'What a show!'
While wave and breeze put on a glow.

With laughter ringing, day feels bright,
In dappled shade, all seems just right.
Together they dance, playful throng,
In the heart of this beachy song.

Secrets Beneath the Canopy

A squirrel's stash of stolen fries,
Beneath the leaves, a great surprise.
He guffaws softly, all alone,
As gulls plot how to steal his throne.

Foliage rustles with secret glee,
As turtles giggle, 'Look at he!'
They gossip tales of beachgoers' slips,
While sand crabs hold their tiny scripts.

A hidden path, a curtain drawn,
Where pranks are played from dusk till dawn.
Laughter hums through every branch,
As breezy whispers start to dance.

The canopy holds its breath, just so,
Waiting for a splash, a funny show.
In leafy shadows, joy ignites,
As nature plays on and delights.

Melodies of Swaying Green

The leaves above began to sway,
To melodies of a sunny day.
A turtle tried to join the tune,
But tripped and fell, much like a goon.

With each sway, secrets are shared,
As sea winds brush and laughter's aired.
A monkey swings by, full of cheer,
Offering jokes, 'Come laugh right here!'

Grasshoppers dance with lively kicks,
Playing tunes on little sticks.
Each bump and wiggle brings a grin,
As nature spins her wild din.

Beneath the sun, they all connect,
In joyful chaos, no defect.
The green stage holds each creature tight,
In melodies that feel just right.

Serenity in Teal and Turquoise

In shades of blue, the laughter flows,
Where dolphins leap and tickle toes.
A parrot squawks, 'What's up, my friend?'
With jokes that twist and never end.

The crabs hold court with sideways flair,
As beach balls bounce and skies are fair.
They dance and jetski in the tide,
With little waves their joyful ride.

The sun dips low, as shadows stretch,
While seaweed wraps like a funny sketch.
They chuckle at each wave's embrace,
In azure hues, a happy place.

With every splash, a giggle rings,
In quiet moments, joy still clings.
Serenity blooms in playful guise,
As everyone revels under skies.

Silhouettes at Dusk

A crooked figure stands so tall,
Did he just trip? Oh, what a fall!
The sunlight bends, it twists and bends,
Who knew that laughter never ends?

A dance of shapes on sandy ground,
While silly jokes are flying 'round.
We mimic seagulls, what a sight,
A funny twist in evening light.

Don't mind that shadow, it's just Fred,
With jellyfish bouncing on his head.
We giggle, snicker, hold our sides,
As evening chuckles, fun abides.

With every fade, the sky gets bold,
While laughter's warmth becomes our gold.
So here's to dusk with crickets' cheer,
In shadows' game, we're all sincere.

Breezes Between the Fronds

A gentle gust, it tickles too,
It made my hat fly—oh, what a coup!
With giggles shared, the breeze helps tease,
As fronds above engage in ease.

Oh look! A squirrel in a bright red tie,
Dancing 'round while we just sigh.
Each little rustle, a whispered jest,
The palm trees know how to jest best.

Let's chase the waves, oh what a plan!
Is that a mermaid? No, just Stan!
With every splash, a laugh spills forth,
As breezes sway in gentle mirth.

So let the whispers blend in fun,
With every laugh, we feel the sun.
Among these leaves, our spirits rise,
In breezy whims, adventure lies.

Coastal Dreams and Silken Layers

In dreams we sail on silks so bright,
While jellyfish wear hats—what a sight!
The ocean sings a tune of glee,
As starfish dance, wild and free.

With flip-flops flying left and right,
We slip and slide, oh what a fright!
A picnic spreads but ah! Too late,
Seagulls swoop; they made my plate!

As shells become our prized displays,
Each tells a tale of silly ways.
With ocean giggles, we spin and twirl,
As waves tease toes, oh what a whirl!

So together we'll sing, draped in cheer,
In coastal dreams, we'll persevere.
With memories bright, and laughter clear,
Our silken layers wrap us near.

Reflections on Sunlit Waves

Oh look—a duck, with shades so neat,
He struts like he's got fancy feet!
Each wave reflects a silly grin,
What fun we find if we just swim.

The ocean foams and tickles toes,
As laughter dances, and everyone knows.
With every splash, a story grows,
In watery worlds, the fun just flows.

A sea star flips, not quite in sync,
While crabs join hands, and don't you think?
With bubbles rising, we hold our breath,
In wave after wave, we laugh our best.

So here's to waters bright and bold,
With tales of laughter yet untold.
In reflections we find our silly fate,
As on these waves, we dance and skate.

Ephemeral Touch of Light

The sun did wink with a playful grin,
As seagulls danced, and crabs joined in.
Sand castles crumbled with laughter loud,
While a ladybug joined the sandy crowd.

A squirrel then tried to wear a hat,
Made of seaweed, it suited him flat.
He strutted around like he owned the day,
While waves rolled in, like kids at play.

A jellyfish twirled in a quirky ballet,
While starfish giggled, 'Get out of our way!'
Even the tide seemed to roll with cheer,
As beach balls bounced, bringing joy near.

And when the sun dipped, the laughter swayed,
In a shimmering glow, the fun never played.
With shadows sprawling across the shore,
The day ended, but we wanted more.

Seashell Melodies

Seashells sang with a cracking tune,
As the tide pulled out like a silver spoon.
They whispered secrets of fish and foam,
To crabs who thought they'd make it their home.

An octopus juggled, oh what a sight!
With shells and starfish, all in delight.
A clam with a crown, so proud and grand,
Declared a kingdom of sand and strand.

A hermit crab wore a bucket, so neat,
Claiming it stylish, to everyone's greet.
He waved at the gulls with a wink and a shout,
"Join in the fun, let's dance about!"

The tide drew closer with a tickling kiss,
While shells laughed louder, "Oh, what bliss!"
As the moonlight shimmered, the beach was aglow,
Ending the night with a seashell show.

Nights Under the Canopy

Under the stars, the laughter arose,
With fireflies winking, in little prose.
A raccoon tried to steal someone's fries,
But tripped on a log, to everyone's surprise!

The crickets chirped in a jazzy beat,
While squirrels busted their best dance feat.
A fox made an entrance, with a top hat on,
Dancing on logs until the break of dawn.

"Let's toast some marshmallows!" a wise owl cried,
While the evening's antics could not be denied.
The trees looked down with a leafy cheer,
Joining the fun, as the night drew near.

With giggles and whispers beneath the trees,
An echoing chorus of "Do as you please!"
As the moonlight faded, and the sky turned blue,
The nights under stars always felt brand new.

Chasing Shadows

Shadows played tag on the golden sand,
With laughter bouncing, oh so unplanned.
A dog ran past, chasing a ghost,
While the sun looked down, not at all engrossed.

Flip-flops flopped like fish out of water,
As conch shells whispered tales that grew hotter.
The sun dropped lower, teasing the day,
While shadows danced in a merry ballet.

A toddler squealed, "Look at my shadow!"
As it twirled gracefully, a tempting meadow.
With giggles and squeaks, the hour grew late,
As shadows partied, sealing their fate.

Then night fell softly, like a cozy hug,
Underneath twinkling stars, so snug.
Our laughter echoed, a fun-filled sound,
As dusk held us close, where joy abounds.

Reflections on Sandy Shores

As waves waltz in the sun's embrace,
Seagulls dance with style and grace.
Sandy toes and laughter loud,
Pretending we're a beachy crowd.

Flip-flops flying like they're free,
A crab runs off—it's just like me!
Sunburned noses, oh what a sight,
We're all just loopy in the light.

Buckets made for castles tall,
But only mud bricks start to fall.
A frisbee lands in someone's drink,
Not a moment to stop and think!

The ocean giggles, tickles our feet,
With every wave, a chance to meet.
So grab your hat, don't lose your way,
Let's savor this beachy play!

Breezes and Dreams

Winds are whipping through my hair,
While seagulls plot from their high lair.
Eating chips while counting flies,
A seagull swoops with sharp intent—oh my!

Sandy sandwiches left to bake,
A crab's eyeing them, a little snake.
With laughter shared like warm sun rays,
We'll dance through this hazy daze.

Drifting dreams on kite strings high,
Just watch that kite—it's in the sky!
A tumble or two when the gusts arrive,
We're just the fools that love to strive.

So grab your board, let's catch some fun,
Not a care—chasing the sun.
With breezes swirling, life's a jest,
In this ocean's embrace, we find our quest!

Ethereal Horizons

What's over there? Just clouds and light,
Voyagers drift, all clean and bright.
With shades of blue that blind the eyes,
Who knew horizons could wear such lies?

While ships sail on clouds made of dreams,
And fishes plot all their schemes.
Unexpected laughter fills the air,
As friends explore without a care.

Naps on boats become a race,
Let's see who wakes up with a face,
In colors bright and giggling tunes,
We'll sing our way to fluffy moons!

The magic hour, a caper spree,
Watch out for crabs—they're all on TV!
With daylight fading, let's lose track,
In this wild world, we won't look back!

Mysterious Tides

The moon's a prankster, don't you see?
It pulls the waves just like a spree.
From jellyfish in polka dots,
To surfers chancing lots and lots.

Time bends funny when it's so late,
Is that a fish or is it fate?
Underwater, secrets whirl and spin,
Where did all their laughter begin?

Tidal pools with treasures rare,
Shells whisper secrets, if you dare.
With each new wave, a splash of fun,
Who knew deep waters could weigh a ton?

Time to dance on a slippery floor,
Careful now—we don't want more.
As tides keep changing, we all glide,
In the ocean's arms—the best ride!

Shimmering Dreams

In a world where fish wear shoes,
And jellybeans laugh at the blues,
A seagull whispers the latest news,
While crabs do the conga, it's all quite a muse.

With sandals that squeak and a hat askew,
The sun's got a joke that we're all in on too,
As the waves play tag, chasing me and you,
We giggle at gulls in their grand, silly queue.

Dancing with shadows, we twirl and we spin,
While starfish cheer us, singing loud like a din,
A crab in a tux does a cheeky little grin,
As we splash in the surf, let the laughter begin.

With each glimmering wave that tickles our toes,
The beach turns a stage for our wacky show,
And as we tumble, the sea foam bestows,
A crown made of laughter that forever glows.

Driftwood Tales

A stick on the shore thought it was a king,
It waved at the gulls, asked, "What do you bring?"
While seashells giggled, each in their own swing,
Telling tales of the waves, and the joy they all cling.

A dolphin named Gerald wore sunglasses so wide,
He flipped and he spun, put his skills to the tide,
With a wink at a crab in a colorful slide,
They all joined in laughter, their worries aside.

The driftwood confesses it misses the trees,
With branches that tickle the cool summer breeze,
But here the sands cheer, and the sunlight agrees,
As drifted-off wood gives its heart to the seas.

Oh, what a gathering of odd wooden things,
With fish dressed as knights and a mollusk that sings,
Each splashing the water as joy softly rings,
In the realm of the silly, where giggling springs.

The Sound of Breeze

The wind gave a huff, then a giggle of glee,
Chasing the kites with a rascal-y spree,
It tickled the sand, and it whispered to me,
Let's spin like a top, oh, wild wind, set me free!

A beach ball bounced high, shouting, "Catch me, please!"
While sea turtles laughed, with shells all at ease,
The sandcastles crumbled, their reign brought to knees,
As we raced with the breeze, a hilarious tease.

Flip-flops do cha-cha, with no care to blend,
Crabs wear bow ties, the ocean's best friend,
In a world full of fun, where silliness bends,
We delight in the twists, let the giggles transcend.

With each wild gust whispering secrets so bright,
The laughter continues, igniting our light,
As waves roll in joy, an exhilarating sight,
We dance with the breeze, through day and through night.

Awakening the Tides

A clam in a tux asked, "What do you say?"
As seagulls debated on who'd lead the play,
The bubbles were gossiping of yesterday,
While jellyfish waltzed in a glittery ballet.

The crabs were on stilts, performing a view,
While waves whispered jokes that only they knew,
An octopus juggled, what a splendid crew,
As we witnessed the antics, all lively and new.

The sand wore a smile, comfy and bright,
Grains dancing in rhythm with pure delight,
Together we laughed at the marvelous sight,
As we stirred up the tides, our spirits took flight.

Oh, let's summon the fun, in this ocean of bliss,
Where waves and the laughter swirl in a kiss,
With seashell applause in the morning's soft mist,
We awaken the tides, on humor we insist!

Whispers of the Tide

Beneath the sun, a beach ball flies,
While seagulls plot their clever lies.
A crab in shades pretends to strut,
And giggles fill the sandy gut.

Sandy toes and squawking tunes,
Juice spills from burst coconuts' prunes.
With flip-flops slapping, we laugh and race,
As tides play tag with a smiling face.

Buckets full of laughter's catch,
Where little waves play hide and snatch.
A jellyfish in a dance-off move,
Makes everyone break into a groove.

As sun dips low, we all unite,
With sunburnt noses in the twilight.
The ocean winks, and we can't resist,
To dive right back into the mist!

Celestial Canopies

Stars above in a twinkling race,
While crickets start a serenade space.
A dolphin hums a catchy tune,
Underneath the giggling moon.

Palm fronds sway in silly dance,
The local lizard's got a chance!
On shoulders perched, they shimmy and sway,
Whispering tales of yesterday.

Cookies crumbled, bats zoom past,
In this wild night, the fun will last.
With glowing lights, the party's on,
Laughing till the break of dawn.

So here we sit, with sand-filled shoes,
Giggling softly at the ocean's muse.
A night of joy, with friends so dear,
Where laughter's echo is all we hear.

Dancing Leaves and Salty Air

On a breezy day, the leaves groove,
With ocean sounds, the heart's in move.
A squirrel's dance on a branch up high,
While ocean breezes seem to sigh.

Nuts in pockets, seashells in hand,
A royal feast upon the sand.
But then a wave, with a splash so bold,
Drags all items from the hold!

The seagull's laughter rings through the chill,
As jellybeans roll down the hill.
A crab in shades has lost its flair,
In a conga line of salty air.

Just when we think the fun must end,
The sun appears, like a trendy friend.
With rays that dance upon the sea,
We all embrace this wacky spree!

Echoes Beneath the Canopy

Under the trees where secrets sleep,
A squirrel's chatter goes so deep.
The dance of leaves, a funny show,
As whispers weave through breezy flow.

A crab in disguise with a hat so wide,
Thinks he's the captain of this tide!
Laughing fish jump, throwing sprinkles high,
While jellyfish float, looking shy.

Mangoes tumble, the ground says 'yow!'
As coconuts plop, it's fun time now!
Lost in laughter, we chase around,
With echoes of joy in this playground.

With giggles bursting, we dive to find,
The silly treasures left behind.
So come, dear friend, and share the thrill,
In nature's joy, our hearts we fill!

Silhouettes of Serenity

In the glow of summer light,
A crab scuttles, oh what a sight!
With a dance that's quite absurd,
Even fish are laughing, it's unheard!

Seagulls glide with cheeky flair,
Stealing snacks from folks who dare.
Why chase waves when you can eat?
Nature's buffet can't be beat!

Turtles nap with silly grins,
While kids play tag with seafoam winds.
A lighthouse winks, it's in on the joke,
As the tide rolls in, making all folks choke!

So gather 'round, let laughter sing,
In the soft warmth of the ocean spring.
The day may end with giggles galore,
And memories made, who could ask for more?

Veils of Sea Breeze

Caught a whiff of salty air,
A sandbar's fond of showing flair.
The breeze just can't resist a tease,
As it lifts away the hats with ease!

The dolphins jump, they're quite the show,
With flips and spins like pros, you know!
But when one lands and splashes near,
It's water fight—the laughter's sheer!

With beach balls flying left and right,
They dodge and weave with pure delight.
An umbrella blooms to catch the sun,
But flips over; now the fun's begun!

So let's raise a toast to wind and tide,
For the shenanigans we can't abide.
The sea may whisper sweet and slow,
But its funny side steals the show!

Dance of the Dusk

As the sun dips down, colors collide,
Flamingos strut, full of pride.
With awkward legs, they seem to sway,
In a dance-off as night claims the day!

Crickets chirp a rhythmic beat,
While frogs join in with their own sweet treat.
A moonlit party, all in jest,
With critters in costumes, looking their best!

Waves shift and giggle, echoing fun,
Seashells sparkle like stars; oh what a run!
A rogue wave crashes, and oh dear me,
Now my flip-flops are swimming at sea!

Let's twirl in the twilight, come what may,
With laughter the language, we play all day.
As the night unfurls its starry cloak,
We'll giggle 'til dawn; who needs a joke?

Shadows Beneath the Canopy

Beneath the branches, shadows creep,
While ants march on, in a line so deep.
A squirrel drops acorns in surprise,
As a butterfly flutters and tries to rise.

A tangle of vines is a simple maze,
Where kids get lost in a curious daze.
The trees gossip, their whispers heard,
Sharing secrets without a word!

A sloth yawns wide, taking his time,
Chasing a leaf, what a funny climb!
While parrots squawk, wearing shades with pride,
In a fashion show, oh what a ride!

So let's twirl, beneath leafy light,
With laughter shared, from day to night.
For nature's playground is wild and free,
And the shadows dance with glee, you see!

The Fabric of Dawn

In the morning light, I tripped on sand,
A crab snickered, waved its clawed hand.
Seagulls giggled, circling near,
While I danced like a fool, full of cheer.

Waves tickled my toes, oh what a tease,
I slipped and fell, splashing with ease.
The sun, like a joker, painted the tide,
As I chased my hat, laughter my guide.

Friends joined in, with their own silly prance,
We all spun around, not a care, but a chance.
To laugh at our clumsiness, joy got us high,
In the fabric of dawn, we all learned to fly.

The ocean winked back, what a sight to behold,
As our jokes grew louder, the sun turned to gold.
In laughter we gathered, hearts soaring like kites,
We danced and we tumbled, till day turned to nights.

Harmony of Elements

The wind blew a whistle, and off we went,
Chasing a wave with a screech and a bent.
Sandcastles crumbled with giggles around,
As we buried our toes, oh what joy we found!

Seashells played tricks, hiding treasures so sly,
While jellyfish bobbed, giving me the eye.
I slipped on a seaweed, spun like a top,
And right into the surf, oh when will it stop?

With splashes and shrieks, the sunlight played tag,
Fish swirled in laughter, their tails doing a wag.
The horizon burst colors, like a painter's wild dream,
While we laughed 'til it hurt, oh what a team!

As elements danced, we joined in the fun,
Mother Nature chuckled; it was a grand run.
Here's to the joys, both silly and bright,
In the harmony found, day turned into night.

Where Land Meets Dream

At the edge where the land seems to sigh,
I found a tall turtle wearing a tie.
He offered me snacks—seaweed and fries,
I questioned his style, but he winked with surprise.

Mermaids threw shade, while dolphins made waves,
They played silly games, showing off their brave.
I joined in the fun, trying flips in the foam,
But landed on my face, oh no, where's my home?

The tide was a riddle, it went in and out,
Like a game of peekaboo, leaving no doubt.
As laughter exploded from sunrise to dusk,
We birthed a new dance, all awkward but husk.

Where dreams flow like water and giggles take flight,
Each tumble and trip was pure delight.
So here's to the whims, the laughter, the gleam,
At the meeting of worlds, we all shared a dream.

Islands of Illusion

On sandy shores where seagulls dive,
A crab wore sunglasses, feeling alive.
He danced to the rhythm of waves so bright,
Claiming he's king on a throne of light.

A coconut fell, and it caused quite a scene,
An octopus wore it like a queen.
With eight graceful legs, she twirled and skipped,
While jealous fish watched, their dreams eclipsed.

Sunburned dolphins with sunscreen mishaps,
Swapped tales of the hardest sea naps.
They giggled and splashed with silly delight,
As a jellyfish tried to put up a fight.

In this land where laughter rides the tide,
Every wave is a joke and a slip on the side.
So join the fun as we splash and play,
In this wacky world where the sun's here to stay.

Twilight's Gentle Serenade

As the sun dipped low, a parrot croaked,
Tales of romance that no one evoked.
His winged buddies laughed, rolling in glee,
Claiming love's simply a fish in a tree.

The crickets chirped in a chorus so loud,
Under the stars, they felt quite proud.
A clam joined in, with a shell of humor,
Saying, "I'm the pearl, but I'm no rumor."

Beneath a big moon, the hermit crabs waltzed,
Twirling in shells that thingamajigs salted.
With laughter unending, they shared a dance,
Silly stuff happens when fish take a chance.

So raise a toast with a smoothie so bright,
Under the glow of this magical night.
For every wave brings a giggle or two,
In this twilight of joy, there's plenty to do.

Silken Waters

In waters so smooth, a fish found a kite,
Swimming in circles, quite a comical sight.
It tangled and flipped, made everyone laugh,
As it tried to glide like a silly giraffe.

A turtle with shades took a leisurely swim,
Singing out tunes that made others grin.
"Who says I'm slow? I'm just playing it cool!"
As he dipped with flair, looking quite the fool.

The seaweed danced to a rhythm of cheer,
Causing a crab to get tangled, oh dear!
He popped up his claws, ready for a fight,
But forgot his own steps, oh what a sight!

So splash in the waves; let's giggle and spin,
In silken waters, we find joy within.
With every chuckle, the day's delight blooms,
As we frolic together in oceanic rooms.

Hushed Secrets of the Shore

The whispers of gulls shared tales of the catch,
While a dolphin declared, "I'm a star, not a batch!"
His flips and tricks drew a crowd on the sand,
As laughing sea turtles formed a dance band.

In the hush of the night, a crab told a joke,
"I'd be a great dancer if I could just poke!"
With two left feet, he managed to sway,
A comedy act, making waves on display.

A starfish sighed, wondering why he was flat,
"Is it wrong to think I should wear a top hat?"
But the waves rolled in, and the seaweed said,
"Just be yourself; it's better instead!"

So let's wander the beach, where laughter's the gold,
In hushed secrets told, the best stories unfold.
With fish and with shells, we'll find our own fun,
In this whimsical world, there's joy for everyone.

Luminous Waveforms

The sea danced bright, so bold and spry,
While fish wore ties and waved goodbye.
Seagulls giggled as they flew,
Stealing fries from folks, who knew!

The crabs lined up for a beach parade,
In tiny hats, they weren't afraid.
Waves laughed loud, splashing in fun,
As sandcastles melted in the sun.

Splashing around, a joyous sight,
While sunbathers fought off the light.
A jellyfish in shades of pink,
Pondered thoughts, made everyone think!

So when you visit, bring a hat,
And make sure to dance with that chatty cat.
The ocean's giggles blend with the breeze,
Count the waves, and just take it easy!

Reflections of Daydreams

On the shore, dreams tumble and roll,
Reflecting laughter, that's the goal.
Mermaids laugh at a sand-filled shoe,
While crabs play tag, not caring who!

Sunbeams tickle the waves so bright,
Creating giggles left and right.
A dolphin dances, twirls with glee,
Winking at swimmers by the sea!

Fishermen drop lines for a laugh,
Instead, they catch a giant gaff.
'No fish today,' they all agree,
Yet seagulls swoop down, as they plea.

Footprints draw stories in the sand,
Of beach ball battles, oh so grand.
Gather round for this silly lore,
And join in on the ocean's roar!

Serpentine Shores

Waves wiggle like a twisty snake,
While sunbathers munch on their cake.
A surfboard flies, crashes with flair,
And someone shouts, 'Don't go out there!'

Flip-flops dance in a frantic chase,
While dogs join in with goofy grace.
Shells gossip beneath sandy skies,
About seagulls with very bad ties!

Chasing crabs down the jiggly trail,
One crab wore glasses, who could fail?
The tide rolls in like a clumsy fool,
Splashing laughter, breaking every rule.

So come join the fun, don't you delay,
At the wiggly shores, come out and play.
Where every wave tells a funny jest,
And the sea's alive, you'll love it best!

Sun-kissed Reminiscences

The sun laughs down with a golden grin,
Surfboards wobble, are they in or out?
Children build castles that sag and lean,
As a toddler starts to shout about!

Funky sunglasses on every face,
As footprints lead to a snacky place.
Ice creams drip like a colorful train,
While seagulls cackle, 'What a gain!'

Turtles surf with a turtle dude,
With boards of lettuce, oh-so-good!
The sunset paints a quirky scene,
Of coconut trees wearing hats so green.

Memories dance on the salty breeze,
As everyone nods and agrees.
Today was a riot, oh what a show,
We'll laugh about it, let the good times flow!

Textures of the Earth and Sea

Waves crash like laughter on rocks,
Seashells giggle in sandy socks.
Fish flip-flop in a comical way,
Making their own little cabaret.

Sunburned tourists, hats askew,
Distracted by seagulls swooping through.
Ice cream drips from sticky hands,
Creating sweet puddles on shifting sands.

Crabs waltz sideways in no rush,
While sandcastles endure a crush.
Jellyfish bounce, looking quite strange,
In a dance only they can arrange.

Under bright skies, the world's alive,
Where silly moments constantly thrive.
A beach ball bounces, tripping a friend,
In this sunny comedy that won't end.

Secrets of Sand and Shade

Beneath the sun, a secret tale,
Of sun hats wearing each other's veil.
Squirrels use shade for a hide-and-seek,
In the game of snack theft, they're quite sleek.

Beach towels debating, which is the best,
While flip-flops frolic, put patience to test.
A seagull snickers from high up a post,
Dropping a sandwich as if to toast.

Crabs have a dance-off, the crowd just roars,
With sand everywhere after built-up scores.
A beach ball whizzes, then gets a new friend,
As laughter rolls on, like waves that don't end.

An umbrella needed a break from the sun,
Decided to cha-cha, oh what fun!
While kids build castles, all tumbling down,
In the kingdom of silliness, without a crown.

Reveries under Woven Skies

Clouds gather in a fluffy debate,
One wears a hat, it looks first-rate.
The sun makes a face, beams of delight,
As kites soar high, a colorful sight.

Seashells whisper, secrets they spill,
About all the wonders, oh what a thrill!
Frogs in a chorus, tuning their song,
In a world where all silly things belong.

The breeze plays tricks, tugging on hats,
As children chase after the colorful mats.
With giggles of joy, they stumble and hop,
Creating a rhythm, will they ever stop?

Underneath skies that twinkle and grin,
The dance of the day is sure to begin.
Where silliness reigns in a twisty charade,
And happiness thrives in each escapade.

Ebbing Currents of Time

Time flows like water, it slips and it slides,
With moments of laughter and silly rides.
Tidepools bubble with fish that converse,
In a language of splashes, it's truly diverse.

Beach games abound, where sand meets the sea,
A frisbee flies, as happy as can be.
Chasing the waves, then dodging the foam,
The beach is a carpet—everyone's home.

As sunsets paint skies with splashes of gold,
Old folks share tales, a bit crazy, quite bold.
They reminisce, while the children jump high,
In a musical moment, with stars in the sky.

And as stars twinkle, it's time to unwind,
With funny stories of the day that was kind.
In a world where laughter is always sublime,
Everything's goofy, in ebbing currents of time.

Echoes of the Tropics

In a hammock, I do sway,
Chasing dreams of sunlit play.
A coconut drops, oh what a thunk,
Where's the party? Oh wait, I'm sunk!

Seagulls squawk, they steal my fries,
Dive-bombing from the bright blue skies.
Sandy toes and silly grins,
When did I lose my sense of wins?

Lemonade spills, just like my brain,
Did I just talk to that iguana plain?
He blinked once, then stole a hat,
Now he's cool, and I look flat!

The sun dips low, a golden splat,
My friends say I've turned into a brat.
With laughter loud and spirits high,
Who knew that sea could make me fly!

Dance of the Seafoam

The waves come in, a bubbly cheer,
With twinkling froth, they seem sincere.
My toes are tickled, what a tease,
Is that a crab or just a sneeze?

A pair of flip-flops lost the race,
Floating off with such great pace.
"Come back!" I yell, "You've got my flair!"
They laugh and dance without a care.

A jellyfish floats by, it's kind of round,
Like my uncle when he hits the ground.
"Don't touch!" they say, but I just grin,
What fun it is to dive right in!

With every splash, my frown takes flight,
I'm the queen of silly, feeling light.
The ocean smiles, it knows my jest,
In foam and giggles, we are blessed!

Tides of Reflection

In moonlit glow, I stand so bold,
Reflections dance, too bright to hold.
What's that in the water? A fish in a suit?
It winks and twirls—what a hoot!

My friends are posing, all shirtless and grand,
"Get the group shot! Perfect!" they planned.
But the tide rolls in with a cheeky grin,
Down they tumble, but I just spin!

Shells hold secrets, they say with a wink,
But do they hold laughs? I need to think.
What if they chuckled at my silly dance?
Then I'd know my luck, oh what a chance!

The ocean's waves, they rush and play,
With every splash, they sweep fear away.
A giggle here, a twist right there,
In mirrored moments, we share a flair!

Dreamy Horizon

Beneath the sky, so vast and wide,
I chase a cloud, what a weird ride!
"Catch me if you can," it seems to say,
But I fall flat, lost in the fray!

Seashell whispers, "You're so great!"
But I just trip, oh what a fate.
Is that a dolphin? Quick, let's wave!
It leaps in joy, so sleek and brave!

A sunset blooms in shades of fun,
Filling hearts before the day's done.
With laughter ringing from coast to coast,
I'll toast a coconut, I'm the host!

In this dreamy place, we laugh and glide,
Against all odds, we take the ride.
With ocean tunes and hearts so light,
We dance till stars show up at night!

Murmurs of the Sea Breeze

Seagulls squawk, they steal my fries,
The ocean whispers, 'Just let it rise!'
Waves tickle toes on this sandy spree,
I blame the gulls, they always tease me.

A crab with swagger, it dances about,
Pinching my flip-flops, what's all this about?
I laugh and I wave, 'You can't take my chair!'
It scuttles away, like it just doesn't care.

The sun acts silly, it bakes my brain,
While jellyfish jiggle, it's quite a strange gain.
The surfboards wobble, as I take a ride,
I'm sure they're laughing, it's hard to hide!

So I sit on the shore with ice cream in hand,
But watch out for gulls – they make their own plans!
With laughter around, fill your cup up with cheer,
For every sweet blunder, a new friend draws near.

Skies of Gossamer Gold

Clouds made of marshmallows are floating up high,
While I chase a kite, oh me, oh my!
The breeze is giggling, tickles my nose,
And here comes a dog, in search of some toes.

A wise old turtle is sunbathing slow,
"Catch me if you can!" he teases, you know?
While children chase bubbles, they laugh with delight,
But they don't see it pop—oh, what a sight!

With toes in the water, my hat takes a dive,
"Don't worry! I told it, this is how we thrive."
The sun's shining bright, making shadows all day,
While seagulls plot mischief in their own little way.

Oh, the sandcastles rise, only to fall,
As waves give them hugs, a watery sprawl.
So I'll laugh at the chaos, dance in the sun,
In skies spun of gold, all's well, it's pure fun!

Swaying Treasures beneath a Mariner's Sun

Nautical knickknacks line up for a show,
A fish in a top hat, what a sight to behold!
Sailboats are twirling, all out of control,
While pirates hold treasure—a jellybean roll!

Flip-flops are flapping, like birds on the run,
I slip on a pair and it shuffles for fun.
Crabs join the conga, they're pulling a prank,
"Hope you can dance!" they wink with a clank.

A bucket of sand gets spilled by a child,
With splashes and giggles, the sea is beguiled.
Sandcastles crumble, but laughter prevails,
As seagulls partake in mischievous tales.

With treasures to find, the day spins around,
In waves of laughter, we all feel profound.
Sun-kissed and salty, we're living it right,
Life's a silly dance—a comical sight!

The Dance of Light and Wave

The sun does a jig on the water so bright,
While fish put on capes, like superheroes in flight.
The shells sing a tune, it's a mariner's tease,
As dolphins do flips, like they aim to please.

A hungry seagull dives, misses its goal,
Splashing in sea foam, it takes quite a poll!
With floats made for children, the sea looks like fun,
But watch for that splash—time to run, everyone!

And here comes a wave, like a giant's big grin,
Catching my toes, it pulls me right in.
With laughter erupting, we dance on the shore,
While the sun rolls along, there's always room for more!

So join in the frolic, embrace every jest,
As light and as wave, we'll dance with the best.
In this sea of laughter, our hearts intertwine,
We're all mariners now, in this grand design!

The Call of Distant Horizons

Breezy whispers dance along,
Sunburned noses sing a song.
Seagulls squawk with all their might,
While tourists spill their drinks in flight.

Flip-flops flop, a creature's cry,
As waves come crashing, oh my, oh my!
Sandcastles tumble, tide steals dreams,
Life's like ice cream, bursting at seams.

Under sunny skies, laughter rings,
Sandy toes do silly things.
A crab scuttles with a quirky strut,
While sunbathers giggle in a peanut rut.

What awaits on shores like this?
A sunburned friend in desperate bliss.
With a splash, it's all in fun,
Adventure calls… let's run, let's run!

Shades of Wilderness

In a forest thick with giggles and squeals,
Frogs in capes wear oddball heels.
Bears try yoga, surrounded by trees,
While raccoons play poker, laughing with ease.

A squirrel in shades, quite the cool dude,
Sips on lemonade, smelling like food.
The wind tells tales of mischief and pranks,
While the owls roll their eyes at the skunks' tired flanks.

Foliage whispers strange jokes to the breeze,
Bringing together critters with ease.
Can you spot the fox in this jolly jam?
He's dressing up as a lost Uncle Sam.

Sunbeams glisten, a narrative wide,
Where the wild things frolic, those critters abide.
With twirls and twitches, they laugh in a row,
How they get along is a magical show!

Secrets in the Surf

Surfboards like dolphins leap and swerve,
While jellyfish float with a twisty curve.
Waves carry whispers from sea to land,
As surf dudes frolic with burgers in hand.

Bikini-clad mermaids chase after snacks,
While sea turtles plot secret attacks.
Seashells gossip, sharing their tales,
Of hidden treasures, and wind-blown gales.

A pelican drops in, what a fine sight,
He steals a chip, such a feathery fright!
With a squawk, he wings it high in the air,
As beachgoers' laughter fills up the square.

Sandcastles rise, with moats around,
Then tumble like ice cream cones on the ground.
Life in the surf sure knows how to sing,
What other secrets will tomorrow bring?

Currents of Calm

Gentle waves whisper humor in sight,
As clumsy otters tumble, what a delight!
Paddleboards wobble, a tale to unfold,
Where giggles and splashes break from the mold.

Seashells play musical chairs on the sand,
While starfish organize a parade so grand.
Sandy snacks scattered, a raccoon's delight,
As the tide rolls in, taking snacks for a flight.

A crab in a top hat offers a dance,
While beach balls bounce in a nonsensical prance.
Flip-flops fly, with laughter ablaze,
Summer's joy wrapped in playful haze.

Laughter spins with the salty air,
Calm vibes cascade, dancing everywhere.
In this arena of fun adrift,
Life's just a game, a whimsical gift!

Murmurs of the Coast

Waves like laughter crash and swell,
Seagulls squawk a sounding bell.
Tip-toeing crabs in party hats,
Dancing sideways, oh, how they prance!

Sandy toes and icy drinks,
The tide pulls in while the sun winks.
Fish flip-flop in a silly spree,
Even seaweed sways in glee.

Umbrellas tumble in the breeze,
Kites get tangled in the trees.
Kids build castles, pails in hand,
Waiting for the tide's sly hand.

So grab your laughter, bring your cheer,
Join the fun, the coast is near!
A goofy dance, a silly twist,
Memories made with an ocean mist.

Celestial Canvas

Stars sprinkle like salt on a cake,
The moon grins wide, oh, make no mistake!
Crickets croon a nighttime tune,
While the waves clap under the moon.

Shells become hats on sandy heads,
The tide's a mad artist with wild spreads.
Brush strokes of foam on the shore,
While laughter echoes, we all roar!

Beach balls bounce like happy dreams,
Underneath the sun's bright beams.
Flip-flops flapping in merry mode,
As we stroll down this giggle road.

So raise a glass to the coastal night,
Where everything feels just so right.
In this silly, shimmering bliss,
Dance with shadows, such a twist!

The Weight of Water

Oh, the ocean's a cheeky thief,
Stealing sandals, a source of grief.
Mom's sunhat goes for a swim,
With every splash, our chances dim.

Buckets splash with giggle-fits,
While dolphins plot their playful bits.
The sea's a jester, what a rogue!
Tickling toes as we all hoag.

A surfboard turns into a kite,
As waves insist on taking flight.
Sandy sandwiches devoured whole,
While waves recite their ocean scroll.

So let's roll in the spoofy tide,
With salty hair, we'll giggle wide.
For in this watery, wacky cheer,
The weight of joy is oh so dear!

A Murmur of Palm Fronds

Wobbly palms wear goofy hats,
Swaying gently with the chats.
Leaves gossip about the breeze,
As squirrels chase them up the trees.

Sunshine spills like syrup warm,
Tiny ants create their swarm.
Fronds rustle like a funny joke,
While turtles watch, and they revoke.

All the creatures in a dance,
Huddling close, they giggle, prance.
Coconuts hold their own debate,
"Who's the funniest? Oh, let's wait!"

So join the furry, hoppy crowd,
Where nonsense reigns and laughter's loud.
Beneath the leaves, find your own thrill,
In this jolly, breezy chill!

www.ingramcontent.com/pod-product-compliance
Lightning Source LLC
Chambersburg PA
CBHW072119070526
44585CB00016B/1507